# MOTORCYCLES
## ON THE MOVE

# MOTORCYCLES
## ON THE MOVE
### A Brief History

9709

LAKE ST. MEDIA CENTER

VERNON, CONN.

JOHN Q. GRIFFIN

Lerner Publications Company ■ Minneapolis, Minnesota

ACKNOWLEDGMENTS: The illustrations are reproduced through the courtesy of: pp. 4, 14, 21, 22, Radio Times Hulton Picture Library, London; p. 7, Deutsches Zweirad-Museum, Neckarsulm, Germany; pp. 8, 16, 19, The Science Museum, London; pp. 25, 26, 28, American Motorcycle Association; pp. 27, 39, 40, 43, 45, 48, 49, Richard Trombley and Gary Hansen; p. 31, U. S. Army; p. 33, Kenneth G. Lawrence's Movie Memorabilia Shop of Hollywood; p. 51, United Press International.

Griffin, John Q.
Motorcycles on the move.

SUMMARY: The history of the motorcycle from the first model built by Gottlieb Daimler in 1885 to the present, including early manufacturing problems and the birth of racing.

1. Motorcycles—Juvenile literature. [1. Motorcycles] I. Title.

TL440.G695 1975        629.22′75        75-17435
ISBN 0-8225-0414-6

Published simultaneously in Canada by J. M. Dent & Sons (Canada) Ltd., Don Mills, Ontario.

Manufactured in the United States of America.

International Standard Book Number: 0-8225-0414-6
Library of Congress Catalog Card Number: 75-17435

4  5  6  7  8  9  10  85  84  83  82  81  80  79

## "GET A HORSE, YOU FOOL!"

Make believe you are living in Germany in the year 1885. There are no telephones, no cars, no airplanes. For all you know, the moon is made of green cheese. When you want to go someplace, you walk. Your father has a horse and buggy, and your uncle in the city has told you about a strange new machine called a "bicycle." People are actually supposed to *ride* on this silly contraption!

Your family lives in the country, on a small green farm. The sun is shining today, and it is quiet and peaceful outside. You have finished all your chores. So you sit down under a tree, to rest for a while. . . .

All at once—you hear loud noises in the distance. Clickety-clack! Snap! Bang! Pop! Clickety-clack! Frightened by the strange sounds, all the cows and chickens start running around in circles. Then, as the noise gets louder, the dogs start barking.

You run over to the dirt road, where the noise seems to be coming from. When you see what's coming down the road, your heart almost stops. You rub your eyes, because you can't believe what you are seeing. A young man is riding on what looks like a wooden horse with two wheels! The wheels are big, like the ones on buggies, and they're turning *all by themselves*! This horse-on-wheels sounds something like a gun going off. But all it "shoots" is a lot of dirty black smoke. Other people run over to look, too. Some of them laugh, but others get angry. One man yells to the young man on the machine, "Get a horse, you fool!"

"Get a horse!" may be what Paul Daimler heard when he rode the first motorcycle ever made. The machine was built by his father, a German engineer named Gottlieb Daimler. The machine's top speed was 12 miles an hour. And it could travel only 3 miles at a time. But it was a beginning.

After Daimler, many men in different countries worked on motorcycles. Today, their work is being carried on by other builders and inventors. This book tells the story of how motorcycles have changed through the years. It takes a look at the motorcycles of today, describing the three major kinds. And it tells what the motorcycles of tomorrow will probably look like.

## GOTTLIEB DAIMLER: FATHER OF THE MOTORCYCLE

It was back in 1885 when Gottlieb Daimler built the world's first motorcycle. He made it by attaching a small gasoline-burning engine to a wooden bicycle frame. The machine had two ordinary carriage wheels, a handlebar for steering the front wheel, and a saddle for the rider to sit on. The engine, or motor, was right under the saddle. It drove the machine by turning a belt connected to the rear wheel. So Daimler's funny-looking "horse-on-wheels" was really just a motorized bicycle—or a "motorcycle."

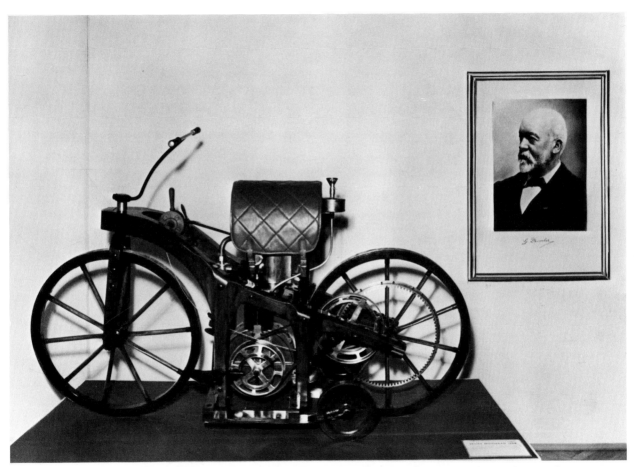
A model of Gottlieb Daimler's motorcycle, with a portrait of Daimler in the background

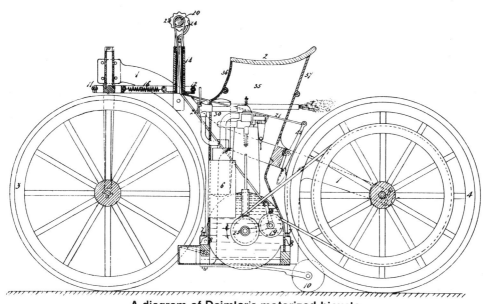

A diagram of Daimler's motorized bicycle

Gottlieb Daimler made only one motorcycle. But he made a number of different engines. The gasoline engine was an exciting new toy to Daimler, and he wanted to see how many ways he could use it to make machines that moved. Some of Daimler's ideas seemed crazy at the time. One day, he put a ski underneath his motorcycle's front wheel. Then he put pieces of metal on the rear wheel, so that it wouldn't slide. After making these changes in his motorcycle, Daimler rode the machine over snow and ice. And so the world's first motorcycle became the world's first snowmobile!

Guess who made the first car? And one of the first motorboats? And the first bus that ran on a track? Gottlieb Daimler made them all! Each of his inventions was a breakthrough, an important first. Yet Gottlieb Daimler is best remembered as the "father of the motorcycle."

## THE EARLY YEARS: PROBLEMS, PROBLEMS, PROBLEMS

Daimler did not want to make and sell motorcycles for a living. But there were other people who did. Unfortunately, making motorcycles was not an easy way to earn a living during those days. Motorcycles were run by engines, and many people did not like engines or machines powered by engines. These machines were loud. They were dirty. They did not work well. They frightened animals, and they frightened people, too.

It is easy to see why people were afraid of motorcycles and other early machines with engines. A machine that moved under its own power was a new idea in the 1880s. "How can a machine run by itself?" people wondered. "Is it alive?" "Does it eat?" "Will it take over the world?" These mechanical monsters seemed very dangerous.

In England, the government passed two laws to try to stop people from making or operating the new machines. These laws were called the "Locomotives on Highways Acts" (a locomotive is a machine that moves by itself). The laws said that a road locomotive had to be operated by at least three drivers. A fourth person had to walk in front of the machine, carrying a red flag to warn people to stay out of the way. What is more, the laws set a maximum speed limit of only four miles an hour for all road locomotives. Anyone who went over the speed limit was to be fined or thrown in jail, or both!

The Locomotives on Highways Acts made it difficult for people in England who wanted to make motorcycles. "How can you build a motorcycle to carry three riders?" they asked. "And why even try if the fastest you can go is four miles an hour?"

Motorcycles were not very popular outside of England, either. But, fortunately, no laws were passed in Europe or America to stop people from making the two-wheeled machines. So work on the early motorcycles went on. . . .

The men and women who made the first motorcycles and cars did not care if their machines were not popular. They were looking into the future, and they saw a world where everyone would have a car or a motorcycle. They knew that someday their machines would make life better. These people said: "Yes, my machine is loud and dirty now. But it is only a baby. All babies are loud and dirty. In a few years my machine will grow up, and then you will see that it can help you. It will not scare you. You will want one yourself!"

The makers of the first motorcycles were right. It was not long before people started to buy their machines. By the early 1890s, motorcycles were becoming popular, and more and more people were making them. They made them simply by putting engines on ordinary bicycles. These early motorcycles were sometimes called "mopeds." The *mo* stands for "motor" and the *ped* stands for "pedal." That's right, the earliest motorcycles had pedals!

The pedals were needed for several reasons. First, they helped to get the motorcycles up hills. The engines were not strong enough to do this job. So when a motorcycle rider came to a hill, he turned off the motor. Then he pedaled his way up the hill. Once he reached the top, he turned on the motor again and rode down the hill—fast!

Pedals also helped when the engines broke down. The earliest motorcycle engines were not very strong or dependable. If a rider could not start his engine, or if the engine broke down, the rider could always depend on the pedals.

Another reason for the pedals was that the first motorcycles often ran out of gas. The engines used on the earliest motorcycles could hold only a small amount of gasoline. And in those days, there were no gas stations. But if a motorcycle ran out of fuel, the rider could always pedal his way home. At times like these, the pedals really came in handy.

Have you ever ridden a bike? It's not hard to pedal down a hill. And it's not too hard to pedal on flat ground. Pedaling *uphill* is the hard part. Well, when you put a heavy engine on a bicycle, it becomes even *harder* to pedal uphill. You might ask, "Why would anyone want a motorcycle that did not go up hills?" The people who made the first motorcycles would answer, "Go ahead, make fun of me. But you'll see. Someday my motor-

cycle will ride up hills as fast as it rides down hills."

It would be quite some time before motorcycle makers could make good this promise. For the first motorcycles had other problems besides weak engines, mechanical breakdowns, and a shortage of gasoline. With their heavy engines and their light bicycle frames, the motorcycles were not very well balanced. They leaned toward wherever the engine was placed, and this made them fall over easily. People tried putting the engine in different places on the motorcycle. Some put it on top of the front wheel. Others put it above the rear wheel. A few people even tried putting the engine under the handlebars or behind the seat! But nothing seemed to work. The early motorcycle makers just could not find the right place for the engine.

The skinny wood-and-iron wheels used on the first motorcycles were another problem. They were better suited to horse-drawn carriages than to motorized bicycles. These carriage-type wheels were hard and wobbly. Along with the heavy engines, they made the first motorcycles fall over a lot. And this made for lots of scrapes and scratches, bumps and bruises.

Unfortunately, the roads made matters even worse. During the early days of motorcycles, most roads were in terrible shape. They were rugged dirt roads meant for horses and buggies—not for motorcycles and cars. These roads had many bumps and holes, and they were covered with rocks and pebbles. When it rained, the roads turned to mud. Horses left big hoofprints in the mud, and carriage wheels left long narrow grooves. When the sun came out and dried the roads, the hoofprints and grooves became hard. This made it even more difficult for people to ride their motorcycles. But they kept on trying!

The first motorcycle riders must have looked very funny. Just imagine it: grown men and women riding wobbly bicycles with noisy engines that sputter and backfire. As the engines speed up and slow down without warning, the riders are jerked backward and forward. The machines teeter from side to side, and the wheels shake and rattle. Whenever the motorbikes hit a bump, they almost fall over on one side. Then, as the riders try to regain their balance, the bikes almost fall over on the *other* side. And all the time the riders are hoping that they won't run out of gas, because it's a long pedal home.

An early motorcycle rider makes her way down a dirt road designed for horse-drawn carriages.

## IMPROVEMENTS ARE MADE

Yes, the first motorcycle riders were a funny-looking lot. But over the years, conditions improved for them. In Germany in 1894, the Hildebrand brothers and their helper, Alois Wolfmuller, built a brand-new motorcycle. They called it the "Hildebrand and Wolfmuller." This motorcycle's top speed was a whopping 24 miles an hour! It had narrow rubber tires, a safety-type bicycle frame, and a powerful water-cooled engine. The new German bicycle still had pedals in case the engine broke down and for use on very steep hills. But it was much better than any motorcycle before it, and it looked more like the motorcycles of today. Many people in both Germany and France bought the Hildebrand and Wolfmuller. In fact, the Hildebrand brothers sold more motorcycles than anyone else at the time.

By the late 1890s, there were enough motorcycles and cars on the road so that people were less afraid of them. This was true even in England. In 1896 England's Locomotives on Highways Acts were done away with. Now the English people could ride motorcycles and drive cars as fast as they wanted to. And only one rider or driver was needed for each machine. For the first time, motorcycles went on sale in England.

An American named E. J. Pennington went to England in 1896 to sell motorcycles. He did not make very good motorcycles. But he tricked many people into buying them. Pennington said that his motorcycles were the best in the world. He even said they could jump over rivers!

**The Hildebrand and Wolfmuller, 1894**

Of course, Pennington's motorcycles could not really jump over rivers—or even over small puddles. But most people in England knew very little about motorcycles, and they believed what Pennington told them. They thought that if a machine could move by itself, it could do almost *anything* (even jump over a river). So E. J. Pennington sold a lot of motorcycles to the English, and he made a great deal of money.

Pennington did almost nothing to help make the motorcycle a better working machine. But he proved that people *could* earn a living by making and selling motorcycles. Between 1896 and 1900, many people in England and other countries began to make and sell motorcycles. As more and more people went into the motorcycle business, more and more improvements were made on the motorcycle. The newer motorcycles were faster, stronger, and sleeker than the ones before. They went up small hills without the help of the pedals, and they didn't fall over quite so often. They still were not very well balanced, due to their heavy engines. But with their air-filled rubber tires, they rode more smoothly than ever before.

In 1900 the first important American motorcycle was made. It was called the "Thomas." It was the first motorcycle to have the engine attached to the bottom of the frame, midway between the front and back wheels. Because the weight of the engine was evenly distributed, it did not tip the motorcycle to one side or the other. The Thomas was a well-balanced motorcycle—a big improvement over earlier ones. But few people knew about the Thomas, and few motorcycle makers copied it.

A landmark in motorcycle history was made one year later, in 1901. That year, the Werner brothers of France built the most important motorcycle since Daimler's. Instead of attaching an engine to an ordinary bicycle frame, the Werner brothers built their engine right into a specially designed motorcycle frame. They put the engine down low on the frame, where the pedals usually went.

And they got rid of the pedals! They did this because they were sure that their single-cylinder engine would always start. And they were sure that it was powerful enough to get their motorcycle up even the highest hill without the need of pedals. The "Werner," as it was called, was not just a motorized bicycle. It was a motorcycle with no pedals. When the pedals came off the motorcycle, it was like the first time you took the training wheels off your bike. The motorcycle had grown up!

The Werner was a great success. The weight of its engine was evenly distributed; so the Werner was a well-balanced machine that hardly ever fell over. And it was much safer and faster than the older motorcycles. Motorcycle racing was just starting as a sport, and the Werner won most of the first races. Many people heard about this speedy new motorcycle and started to buy it. Soon everyone who made motorcycles was copying the Werner.

After the Werner, motorcycles kept getting bigger, faster, and more powerful. Wider rubber tires were made especially for motorcycles. They helped make the machines safer, for they gripped the road better than the skinny rubber tires of earlier days. They did not slip on turns or tip over on bumps.

Over the years, the engines built for motorcycles became larger and more powerful. They went from less than two horsepower to more than five horsepower. One horsepower is the amount of power made by one horse. So a motorcycle with a five-horse-

Built in 1901 by the Werner brothers, the Werner was the most important motorcycle since Daimler's.

power engine has the same power as a motorcycle pulled by five horses.

By 1905, some motorcycles could go 60 miles an hour. These were special racing bikes built only for speed. But even ordinary motorcycles were able to go 30 or 40 miles an hour. The frames built for these bikes were made stronger, to hold the heavier engines. Headlights and speedometers were added to the motorcycles to make them safer. For the first time, motorcycle riders could see in the dark and tell how fast they were going.

By 1906, people no longer laughed at motorcycles. They were not afraid of them any more, either. People had finally gotten used to the idea of machines that made their own power. In fact, they liked the new machines. They would say: "Motorcycles sure make travel easier. They pull heavy loads at high speeds, and they are fun to drive. And just think, one little motorcycle has the power of five big horses! What will they think of next?" Gottlieb Daimler and all the others had been right. Men and women *did* learn to love motorcycles and cars. The men who had been called "fools" were now being called "heroes."

## EARLY MOTORCYCLE RACING

There were other heroes besides the pioneers who built the first motorcycles. Motorcycle racing had become a popular sport, and the men who raced motorcycles were cheered on by large crowds of spectators. There were two important kinds of motorcycle races. The

A racer stands beside his American-made "Indian" motorcycle before the start of a track race, 1911.

Two long-distance racers fight it out for first place in the Isle of Man Tourist Trophy Race, 1913.

first kind was run on a flat, oval-shaped racing track less than half a mile long. Special motorcycles were built just for these races. The track-racing bikes did not have to be able to go over rough roads or up steep hills. They just had to go *fast*, covering a short, flat racing track in as little time as possible. To increase their speeds, most of these motorcycles had huge high-powered engines.

The second kind of motorcycle race was the long-distance race. These exciting contests were run over rough roads and up and down steep hills. The riders raced ordinary motorcycles, just like the ones everyone else could buy. These bikes did not go as fast as the high-powered machines built for track racing. But they were a lot tougher, and they were able to ride over all kinds of roads safely.

The most famous long-distance race was held on the Isle of Man, a small island off the coast of Scotland. This race was called the Isle of Man Tourist Trophy Race. It was started back in 1907, and it is still going strong today. The first Isle of Man race was won by an English bike called the "Norton." The Norton's top speed was 43 miles an hour. It won the big race with an average speed of 36 miles an hour—not bad for such a rugged long-distance event.

Over the years, the Isle of Man Tourist Trophy Race became the most important motorcycle race of all. Motorcycle riders from all over the world tried to win the trophy for this top race. But there were other motorcycle races to compete in, and other trophies to win. Almost all the companies who made motorcycles entered the big races. They knew that if they won, they would become famous. And they were sure that if they became famous, lots of people would buy their motorcycles and they would become very rich. So each motorcycle company tried to outdo the other one, building a faster, more powerful machine.

An English motorcycle called the "Douglas" set a new world speed record of 80 miles an hour in 1914. Motorcycles had become very popular in England by then. They had also become popular in France, Germany, and many other European countries. But America was the land of the motorcycle. More people made and rode motorcycles in America than anywhere else in the world.

In 1914, when World War I started in Europe, motorcycle racing stopped there. About the only motorcycles made in Europe were those that were sold to the armed forces for military use. In 1917, when America entered the war, motorcycle racing stopped there, too. America continued to make thousands of motorcycles, but these bikes were not for racing or for pleasure riding. They were made for the United States Army and for the armies of England and France.

The cyclist in this photo is demonstrating his riding skill on an off-the-road motorcycle, or trail bike.

Big road motorcycles like this touring bike are well suited for long trips on the highway.

A young cyclist rides along a wooded trail on a minibike, a small off-the-road motorcycle with a tiny engine.

Motorcycle racers compete in the 1975 Daytona 200. This thrilling race is one of the 7,000 motorcycle events sponsored by the American Motorcycle Association, which was founded in 1924.

## AFTER WORLD WAR I:
## FASTER BUT NOT MUCH BETTER

After World War I ended in 1918, motorcycles were no longer very popular in America. The land of the motorcycle was rapidly becoming the land of the car. For the first time in history, large numbers of cars were being built on assembly lines. American-made cars were getting cheaper and better all the time. And they were bigger, safer, and more comfortable than motorcycles. So not many people in America wanted to buy motorcycles any more. They wanted cars! Only two of the American companies that had been making motorcycles before the war were still making them after the war. One was the Harley-Davidson Company, which is still the top-ranking motorcycle company in America. The other was the Indian Company, whose well-built "Indians" were among the best and most popular motorcycles ever made.

In America, the people wanted cars, cars, and more cars. But in England and Europe, motorcycles were still very popular. As America became the leading maker of cars, England became the leading maker of motorcycles. By 1919 there were more than a hundred motorcycle companies in that country. And each of them turned out hundreds of motorcycles, flooding the market with the two-wheeled machines.

Motorcycle racing came back stronger than ever after the war. Many new racing events were established, and many new speed records were set. In 1921 the winner of the Isle of Man Tourist Trophy Race reached a top speed of 74 miles an hour. Four years later, a lightning-fast English motorcycle called the "Brough Superior" set a new world speed record of 123 miles an hour. That record was broken in 1936 by a German-made motorcycle. The bike's top speed was an amazing 169 miles an hour!

Motorcycles were getting faster all the time. But after World War I, there were few important changes in the way motorcycles looked. Most of the big changes and improvements had already been made. Along with headlights and speedometers, motorcycles now had wider tires, more comfortable seats, and more dependable brakes. They also had better mufflers, or "silencers," and so were not as noisy as before. Their frames were stronger, their fuel tanks larger, and their engines more powerful. But no new types or styles of motorcycle frames were designed; and no new kinds of engines were invented. The motorcycles of the 1930s looked much like the ones built before the First World War.

In 1939, when World War II broke out, thousands of motorcycles were again built for military use. It was like World War I all over again. The making of motorcycles for

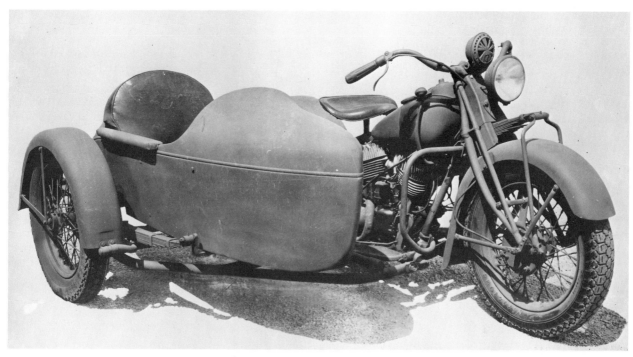

U.S. Army cycle with sidecar, 1942

pleasure and sport stopped while men and women went to war. Most of the military motorcycles made during the Second World War were big, heavy, and rugged. Some had machine guns mounted on their frames, and some had sidecars to carry soldiers in. Motorcycles were used by military police, by medical corpsmen, and by ammunition carriers. They were also used by "dispatch riders"—or message carriers—who had to get around war zones and across rough, battle-scarred areas in a hurry.

## AFTER WORLD WAR II:
## THE WORST SLUMP YET

After the war ended in 1945, the motorcycle business suffered its worst slump yet. Few people were buying motorcycles any more. Cars had become popular in England and Europe, just as they had in America. And for the first time, large numbers of them were being made and sold outside the United States. Cars were safer and more comfortable than motorcycles, and they could carry passengers. They kept the driver and passengers warm when it was cold out, and dry when it was wet. Most people thought that only a racer or a fool would pick a motorcycle over a car.

Motorcycles were fighting a losing battle against cars. And for a while, it seemed as if the two-wheeled vehicles were on their way out. Many motorcycle companies, including the Indian Company in America, were forced to close down. And the ones that stayed in business turned out fewer motorcycles than ever before.

Most of the motorcycles built after the war were big, fast, and expensive. Some of these bikes were sold to police departments and used by traffic officers. But a great many more were sold to racers. Motorcycle racing was still a popular sport in the late 1940s, and the newer bikes often hit speeds of more than 100 miles an hour. But by the late 1950s, motorcycles were more unpopular than ever with the general public. Many people looked down on motorcycles, calling them loud, dirty, and dangerous. Only troublemakers and gang members rode motorcycles, they thought.

These ideas about motorcycles were shown in the movie *The Wild One*, starring Marlon Brando. All the motorcycle riders in this movie were young, tough, and "wild." They wore black-leather jackets, and they drank too much beer. They were a pack of hell raisers who took over a small town, breaking the law and making fun of helpless old people.

Many people who saw the movie believed that *all* motorcycle riders were like the ones in *The Wild One*. Of course, people knew that policemen rode motorcycles, too. But motorcycle gangs like the Hell's Angels of California drew a lot more attention, and they gave the motorcycle a bad name. As a result, motorcycle riders were not well liked. Most law-abiding citizens called them "hoods."

**Marlon Brando in *The Wild One***

## HONDA: THE MAN
## AND THE MACHINE

People's ideas about motorcycles and motorcycle riders were soon to change. The change was brought about by a Japanese man named Soichiro Honda. Mr. Honda had been a motorcycle racer and mechanic before World War II. In 1945, after Japan lost the war, he started to build mopeds (motorcycles with pedals). He bought 500 old gasoline engines that had been used by the Japanese army during the war. And he fitted these engines onto ordinary bicycles. Honda's motorized bicycles did not run very well. But they were cheap, and they were the only motorcycles being made in Japan at the time. Honda sold every motorcycle he built.

Before long, Mr. Honda used up all the engines he had bought from the army. So he started to build his own engines, putting them on bikes. These small motorcycles were a lot like the ones that had been built during the 1890s. They were nothing like the big powerful motorcycles being made in Europe and America. In fact, they weren't really motorcycles: they were bicycles with engines. But they were cheap, and they sold very well.

In 1948 Mr. Honda used all the money he had made to start building *real* motorcycles. Instead of putting engines on bikes, he put his engines into small lightweight motorcycle frames. Honda was so successful that in 1952 the Japanese government lent him $1 million. Mr. Honda used this money to build large factories where thousands of small motorcycles, or "Hondas," could be made.

**A 1948 Honda motorcycle**

In 1957 Honda sold a grand total of five motorcycles to people living in countries other than Japan. These were the *first* Hondas sold outside of Japan. In 1960 Mr. Honda started to sell his lightweight motorcycles to people living in America. Until then, the only motorcycles sold in America had been big, fast, and expensive. Soichiro Honda believed that Americans were ready for a new kind of motorcycle. His bikes were small, light, and inexpensive. And they were cheap to operate, for they did not use much gasoline. As it turned out, Soichiro Honda was right. Americans *were* ready for a new kind of motorcycle, and the Honda fit the bill.

The Honda Motor Company sold motorcycles to all kinds of people, not just to racers. Businessmen, housewives, lawyers, students, and doctors—they all wanted Hondas. With so many cars on the road, small motorcycles made sense. They did not cost much to buy or to run, and they were easy to handle. Because they were so small, they could zigzag through heavy traffic without any trouble. And they were just right for short trips to work or to school or to the store.

Soichiro Honda's lightweight motorcycles performed well on streets and roads. But they were not tough enough or strong enough to be used in places where no roads existed. Before long, though, the Honda Motor Company started to make specially designed motorcycles for off-the-road riding and exploring. These bikes could be used on trails and paths, in forests and woodlands. Many people bought the new off-the-road machines. They were tougher and more powerful than ordinary Hondas. And they made it easy for people to get away from the city and its crowds.

In 1962 the Honda Motor Company sold more than 1 million motorcycles. Although many of these bikes were sold in America, the people of Japan bought more Hondas than anyone else. But five years later, in 1967, over 600,000 Hondas were sold *outside of Japan*. Most of these bikes were sold in the United States. The Honda had become the most popular motorcycle in America. And Soichiro Honda's little company had become the largest and most important motorcycle company in the world.

## THE NEW POPULARITY OF MOTORCYCLES

Thanks to Mr. Honda, the motorcycle had become popular again. Only this time it was popular with average, everyday people as well as with racers. By 1970 there were dozens of new motorcycle companies in business. And people now had many different sizes and types of motorcycles to choose from. For as the Honda Motor Company started to make bigger bikes, Harley-Davidson and other companies started to make smaller ones.

After the energy crisis started in 1973, motorcycles became even more popular. Unlike cars, they could go a long way on just two or three gallons of gasoline. And besides the savings in fuel, they cost only a fraction of what cars cost. As a result, more and more people turned from cars to motorcycles as their main means of transportation. This was true not only in the United States, but also in England, France, Germany, Italy, and Japan. All the dreams and hopes of Gottlieb Daimler had been realized. The motorcycle had grown up, and it was here to stay.

## THE MOTORCYCLES OF TODAY

Today—less than 100 years after Daimler built the first motorbike—there are so many different makes and models of motorcycles that it's difficult to tell them all apart. But there are three basic types or classes of motorcycles. Each type of bike is designed for a different purpose, and each has something that the others lack.

First, there are the *road motorcycles*. These bikes are designed for use on roads, highways, city streets, and other paved surfaces. All road motorcycles are required by law to have headlights, taillights, brake lights, rearview mirrors, horns, and other standard safety equipment. Road bikes are bigger and more comfortable than other motorcycles.

They are also heavier and more powerful. Some road motorcycles are fast enough to reach the same speeds as cars. And because they have large fuel tanks, they can go a long way between stops.

*Off-the-road motorcycles* make up the second class of bikes. These motorcycles are often called "trail bikes" because they are designed for use on rough country trails and in places where there are no roads. Trail bikes are neither as heavy nor as fast as road motorcycles, and their fuel tanks are smaller. The exhaust pipe of an off-the-road cycle is mounted high on the frame so that it won't hit the ground when the bike goes over bumps and rocks. And the front fender is

Like all road cycles, this middleweight street bike has mirrors, lights, and other safety equipment.

This close-up of a trail bike gives a good view of the raised fenders and knobby tires found on all off-the-road motorcycles.

usually high above the wheel so that it won't become clogged with mud.

Unlike road motorcycles, off-the-road cycles do not always have horns, mirrors, lights, and other safety equipment needed on roads. But they have special heavy-duty tires with big knobs that grip the dirt. These tires are called "knobbies," and they set trail bikes apart from all others.

There is a third class of motorcycles that can be used *both on and off the road*—on city streets and country trails alike. The bikes in this class are known as *street-scramblers*. They are not as good for street and highway riding as road motorcycles. And they are not as good for trail riding as off-the-road cycles.

But they can do both jobs quite well. Street-scramblers have the same safety equipment found on road motorcycles. And, as with trail bikes, their exhaust pipes are mounted high on the frame to protect them from bumps and rocks. All-around bikes, street-scramblers are designed for cyclists who want to be able to go anywhere.

## WHICH BIKE IS BEST FOR YOU?

There are only three basic types of motorcycles, but each one comes in many different sizes, weights, and models. Some have small lawnmower-type motors of only 5 horsepower. Others have huge engines of 50 horsepower or more. So if you're thinking about getting a motorcycle, you'll find that there are dozens of different kinds to choose from.

Which bike is best for you? That depends on where you want to ride your motorcycle once you get it. If you'll be riding on streets, roads, and highways, then a road motorcycle is the answer for you. But before you can operate a road cycle, you *must* have a driver's license. In most states, you have to be at least 16 years old in order to get a driver's license. And in some states, a driver's license won't do: you need a special motorcycle license in order to operate a road motorcycle. To get the license, you must pass a motorcycle-riding test similar to the ones that car drivers take to get their driver's licenses.

If you do not have a license, then you cannot ride a road motorcycle. But you do not need a license to ride an off-the-road motorcycle. If trail riding is what interests you, then you should get a trail bike. But what kind? Remember, you have to be pretty big to ride a motorcycle. Your legs must be long enough to reach the footrests. And you must be heavy enough to guide the motorcycle into turns. (You help to steer a motorcycle by leaning with all your weight when you turn.) Does this mean that you will not be able to ride a trail bike just because you are short and skinny? No, it does not.

Maybe the best motorcycle for you is a "minibike." A minibike is a small off-the-road motorcycle with small knobby tires and a small engine. It is not as long or as high as

Wearing helmets, gloves, and boots, two trail riders pose on minibikes made by the Honda Motor Company.

other bikes, and it is much lighter. All these things make a minibike easier to handle than most other bikes. And they explain why minibikes are so popular with young and beginning cyclists.

It is against the law to ride a minibike on public roads, for the bike is not equipped for road use. Minibikes are trail bikes, remember, and they are designed only for off-the-road riding. Some cyclists like to ride their minibikes in fields, but this is not a good idea. For even a small motorcycle like a minibike can harm and destroy plants. And the noise it makes can disturb both animals and people. So it is best not to ride in fields and meadows.

It may seem as if there are few places where you can ride a minibike without either breaking the law or bothering someone. But this is not really true. Most cities have special off-the-road riding areas where children can ride minibikes. These are excellent places for beginning riders to learn how to handle their machines. If you live in the country, you can ride a minibike on trails and paths. Or you can ride it on private roads such as the ones leading into farmhouses and lake cabins. (Of course, if the roads are not on your own property, you must ask the owners for permission to ride on them.) Before you go out on your own, though, be sure to have someone give you riding lessons. And whenever you ride, be sure to wear a safety helmet. It is also a good idea to wear gloves, boots, and long pants.

You may be surprised to learn that minibikes are not just for children. Many grown-

Large trail bikes like this one can travel over rugged areas where no roads exist.

ups ride them, too! Some people take mini-bikes along on camping trips. And others enjoy riding them in their own backyards—especially if their backyards are big and open.

There are several different kinds of off-the-road motorcycles, and the minibike is only one of them. When your legs get longer and your body gets heavier, you may want to get one of the larger, more powerful trail bikes. Some trail bikes weigh up to 250 pounds and go as fast as 70 miles an hour. These bikes are used mainly for dirt-track racing. Unless you plan to race, a small or medium-size trail bike should have more than enough power and speed for you.

Maybe you're not interested in trail riding. Maybe you want a motorcycle that you can ride on streets and roads and highways. Then you should get a road motorcycle (provided that you're old enough to get a license, that is). There are three different kinds to choose from: "lightweight street bikes," "touring bikes," and "middleweight street bikes." All three kinds of road motorcycles have headlights, horns, mirrors, and other safety equip-

ment. But they vary greatly in terms of size, weight, power, and speed.

As their name suggests, lightweight street bikes are small road motorcycles designed for street riding. They do not cost very much, and they go a long way on a small tank of gas. Lightweight street bikes are good for riding in town because they can keep up with city traffic and are easy to handle. But they are too slow to keep up with highway traffic, and should not be run at their top speeds for long periods of time. Lightweight street bikes are best for going to and from school or work. If you live in a big town and do not want to take your motorcycle on long trips, then a lightweight street bike is the motorcycle for you.

Touring bikes are heavyweight road motorcycles designed for long trips on the highway. They are big, fast, and comfortable. These monsters weigh up to 900 pounds and can travel up to 100 miles an hour. They are more powerful than other cycles, and can carry heavier loads. (Two riders and their suitcases can easily fit on one of these machines.) Touring bikes are not as easy to handle as smaller motorcycles, though, and they're not as good for street riding. But if you want a powerful bike designed for long trips on the highway—and if you have a lot of money to spend—then a touring bike is right for you.

Middleweight street bikes are in the middle. These road motorcycles weigh up to 350 pounds and reach speeds of up to 80 miles an hour. They are not as small or as easy to steer as lightweight street bikes. And they are not as heavy or as comfortable as touring bikes. They cost more than lightweights but less than touring bikes. If you want a motorcycle that you can use in the city and for short trips in the country, then a middleweight street bike is the best bike for you.

Maybe you want a motorcycle that will go in the city and on the highway, a motorcycle that will go both on and off the road. Maybe you want all this in a motorcycle that does not cost very much. Then you want a street-scrambler. Street-scramblers do all the things that road motorcycles and trail bikes do, but they are not the best for any of them. They are good motorcycles for beginners because

*Left*: This cyclist owns a touring bike, the biggest and fastest motorcycle on the road.

*Right*: A street-scrambler charges through a mudhole. Unlike other motorcycles, street-scramblers can be used both on and off the road.

they are designed for every kind of motorcycle riding.

After deciding which type and kind of motorcycle you want, you must then decide whether to get a new or a used one. Used motorcycles cost less than new ones, of course, but they do not last as long. Whatever you decide on, always test-ride a motorcycle before buying it. Be sure it feels good to you. And talk to motorcycle mechanics, dealers, and experienced riders. Find out from them which motorcycles are built the strongest. Then buy the one that best fits your special needs and desires.

## THE MOTORCYCLES
## OF THE FUTURE

You know quite a bit now about the motorcycles of the past and the present. But what about the motorcycles of the future? What will they look like? Will they still run on gasoline 10 years from now, or will they run on boiling water like Evel Knievel's cycle?

People have made and are making motorcycles that run on electricity. You plug them in at night, and then ride them the next day. They don't need gas, and they don't have to be fixed as often as regular motorcycles. Maybe all the motorcycles of the future will run on electricity.

But there is another kind of motorcycle that is being made now. It is small, light, and fun to ride. It doesn't cost much, and it doesn't make much noise. It's cheap to operate, because it goes a long way on a tank of gas. And it can run without its engine, because it has pedals. That's right, it's a moped, a bicycle with a motor! Strange as it may seem, the motorcycles of the future may be like the ones made back in the 1890s . . . and the ones built by Soichiro Honda right after World War II. The more things change, it seems, the more they stay the same!

This steam-powered bike may be the motorcycle of the future!

**Superwheels & Thrill Sports**

AMERICAN RACE CAR DRIVERS
INTERNATIONAL RACE CAR DRIVERS
THE DAYTONA 500
THE INDIANAPOLIS 500
AIRPLANE RACING
DRAG RACING
ICE RACING
ROAD RACING
TRACK RACING

MOPED MANIA
MOTORCYCLE RACING
MOTORCYCLES ON THE MOVE
MOTOCROSS MOTORCYCLE RACING
GRAND NATIONAL CHAMPIONSHIP RACES
THE WORLD'S BIGGEST MOTORCYCLE RACE:
    THE DAYTONA 200
YESTERDAY'S MOTORCYCLES
BICYCLE ROAD RACING
BICYCLE TRACK RACING
BICYCLES ON PARADE
SNOWMOBILE RACING

SKYDIVING

AUTO BRIGHTWORK
CLASSIC SPORTS CARS
DINOSAUR CARS: LATE GREAT CARS
    FROM 1945 TO 1966
KIT CARS: CARS YOU CAN BUILD
    YOURSELF
HOME-BUILT AIRPLANES
VANS: THE PERSONALITY VEHICLES
YESTERDAY'S CARS
YESTERDAY'S FIRE ENGINES

Lerner Publications Company

241 First Avenue North, Minneapolis, Minnesota 55401

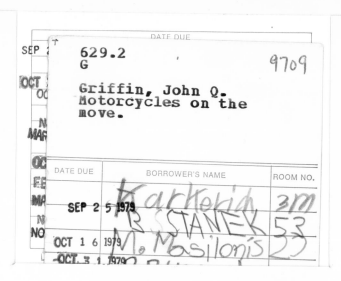